LEROY ANDERSON

AT THE PIANO

COMPLETE WORKS FOR SOLO PIANO

CENTENNIAL EDITION

Copyright © MMVIII by Alfred Publishing Co., Inc.
All rights reserved. Printed in USA.

Cover art by Isabel Wadsworth

ISBN-10: 0-7390-4663-2
ISBN-13: 978-0-7390-4663-0

LEROY ANDERSON
AT THE PIANO
Complete Works for Solo Piano
Centennial Edition

Contents

Foreword

Leroy Anderson's music has long been recognized for its imaginative brilliance and superb craftsmanship. Leroy Anderson, known for his short orchestral compositions, also made arrangements of his works for concert band and other ensembles.

The care and dedication that Anderson brought to the writing of his symphonic works extended to the piano solo editions of his music. He made each of the piano transcriptions of his orchestral pieces in this album.

While Anderson wrote his music for full symphony orchestras to perform, one piece, *Forgotten Dreams*, was composed for piano and orchestra. The opening and closing measures show off the piano's expressiveness.

This book of piano solos includes two pieces that are being published for the first time: *Governor Bradford March*, originally written for orchestra, and *An Old-Fashioned Song*, written for beginning piano students.

Leroy Anderson in the 1950s

Biography

"Leroy Anderson is one of the great American masters of light orchestral music. Though we have performed his works countless times over the years, at the Boston Pops, his music remains forever as young and fresh as the very first day on which it was composed."

— *John Williams, composer,*
Laureate Conductor, Boston Pops

Leroy Anderson, America's preeminent composer of light concert music, wrote such lively and evocative Pops orchestral favorites as *Sleigh Ride*, *The Syncopated Clock* and *Blue Tango*. His music captures the imagination of millions of people around the world with its memorable, optimistic melodies and impeccably crafted orchestrations.

This unassuming composer was born in Cambridge, Massachusetts in 1908, to Swedish immigrant parents. He received his first music lessons from his mother who was a church organist. At age eleven he began piano studies at the New England Conservatory of Music. For his high school graduation he composed, orchestrated and conducted the class song. Anderson attended Harvard University where he received his B.A. (magna cum laude) and M.A. in music, studying with composers Walter Piston and Georges Enesco.

His musical interests included the double bass, trombone, tuba, organ, arranging and conducting. He studied double bass with Gaston Dufresne of the Boston Symphony Orchestra, and organ with Henry Gideon of Boston. At the same time he was the organist and choirmaster of a church in Milton, Massachusetts. When he was in his last year as an undergraduate at Harvard he became the director of the Harvard University Band, then resumed this post in 1931 and began writing arrangements for the band, arrangements held in high regard and still played today by the band.

In 1936 George Judd, manager of the Boston Symphony Orchestra, asked him to make an arrangement of Harvard songs for the Boston Pops to play and thus came to the attention of Arthur Fiedler, music director of the Pops. Fiedler encouraged Anderson to write original works for the Pops. Anderson brought his first work, *Jazz Pizzicato*, to Fiedler in 1938. The Pops then premiered it and from then on he wrote a steady stream of his miniature orchestral masterworks.

During World War II, Leroy Anderson's proficiency in German and Scandinavian languages led him to serve in the Army Counter-Intelligence Corps. He attained the rank of Captain, serving as Chief of the Scandinavian Desk of Military Intelligence at the Pentagon. While at the Pentagon he wrote *Promenade* and *The Syncopated Clock*. At the end of the war he

Leroy Anderson at home in 1952.

Leroy Anderson died of cancer on May 18, 1975, in Woodbury, Connecticut, his home of 25 years.

declined an offer to become the assistant military attaché in Stockholm; instead, he continued his musical career.

Anderson conducted his own orchestra for Decca Records from 1950 to 1962. His popularity as a composer was at an unprecedented high. Never before had a symphonic composer been given an orchestra to conduct and record freshly written music. He gave the first performances of many pieces when he recorded them.

While Anderson's aim was to write light concert music to be played by symphony orchestras, in 1952 *Blue Tango*, a lilting instrumental with a sweeping melody, became the "top single." It was at the top of the Hit Parade for 22 weeks and was played in jukeboxes and on radio in the U.S. and Europe. Anderson's own recording of it earned him a gold record, which was unprecedented for an instrumental symphonic recording.

One of the highlights of his career came in 1972 when he appeared on *Evening at Pops*. This nationally–televised PBS program featured The Boston Pops Orchestra and its conductor Arthur Fiedler. Anderson reminisced that when he first went to a Boston Pops concert while in high school he little knew then that years later "I would be first an arranger and orchestrator for the concerts and then later the composer of some of the music on the programs."

Though Leroy Anderson is best known for his many popular short pieces, he also wrote the music for the Broadway show *Goldilocks* and composed a piano concerto.

Anderson wrote the music for Jean and Walter Kerr's musical *Goldilocks* that opened on Broadway in 1958. Don Ameche and Elaine Stritch starred in the show, which ran for 161 performances. Anderson's delightful score has been enjoyed over the years on the original Broadway cast recording that was reissued on CD in 1992.

Leroy Anderson at home in 1971.

Leroy Anderson with Arthur Fiedler before a 1954 Boston Pops concert with both conducting. The concert was at the 25th reunion of Leroy Anderson's Harvard class of 1929.

Leroy Anderson (1908–1975)

"Leroy Anderson's music has thrilled millions of Americans and indeed the entire international music world for over sixty years."

— *Erich Kunzel, conductor*

1908 June 29, born in Cambridge, Massachusetts to first-generation Swedish parents.

1919 Began piano and music studies at New England Conservatory of Music.

1925 Composed, orchestrated and conducted the Cambridge High and Latin School orchestra in the class song for his graduation; entered Harvard College, studied harmony with Walter Spalding, counterpoint with Edward Ballantine, canon and fugue with William C. Heilman, and orchestration with Edward B. Hill and Walter Piston.

1926 Played trombone, Harvard University Band (through 1929).

1929 Awarded a B.A. magna cum laude in Music from Harvard College; elected to Phi Beta Kappa; continued in Graduate School, studied composition with Walter Piston and Georges Enesco; studied organ with Henry Gideon and double bass with Gaston Dufresne of the Boston Symphony Orchestra.

1930 Awarded an M.A. in Music from Harvard University; tutor, Division of Music, Radcliffe College; continued in Graduate School with studies in German and Scandinavian languages (through 1934).

1931 Director of Harvard University Band (through 1935).

1936 Arranged and conducted *Harvard Fantasy*, a medley of Harvard songs, his first arrangement for the Boston Pops Orchestra; moved to New York City.

1938 *Jazz Pizzicato* premiered by Arthur Fiedler and the Boston Pops.

1942 Married Eleanor Firke; entered U.S. Army, served in Iceland; later Chief of Scandinavian Desk, Military Intelligence Service, Washington, D.C., released as Captain in 1946.

1945 Conducted the Boston Pops in premieres of *Promenade* and *Syncopated Clock*.

1946 Orchestrator and arranger for the Boston Pops (through 1950).

1949 Moved to Woodbury, Connecticut with his wife and children.

1950 First recording session for Decca Records; recorded his own works, often in their first performances, until 1962.

1952 Received gold record for one million sales of his recording of *Blue Tango*.

1954 Conducted his music with the Boston Pops, and other orchestras in the U.S. and Canada (through 1974).

1958 *Goldilocks*, his only musical, opened October 11 in New York City.

1975 May 18, died in Woodbury, Connecticut.

1988 Elected posthumously to the Songwriters Hall of Fame.

1995 Harvard University named new band quarters Anderson Band Center in honor of Leroy Anderson.

2003 Leroy Anderson Square dedicated at composer's boyhood home—12 Chatham Street—in Cambridge, Massachusetts.

Leroy Anderson at home in 1953.

About the Music

"It's very clear that the impact of Mr. Anderson's music, both when it was written and in today's frantic world, is impossible to measure."

— *Leonard Slatkin, conductor*

Arietta (1962) The main melody was first written as a brief eight-measure sketch for viola and cello with Anderson playing cello and his daughter, Jane, playing viola. He then expanded it into a full work in classical two-part form. Since it was lyrical like an aria, but short, he called it *Arietta*.

Balladette (1962) Anderson has woven a simple, lyrical melody around a chromatic ostinato figure in the middle voice.

Belle of the Ball (1951) During a concert, Anderson said: "Composers generally have a whole lot of music lying around that they haven't used. I understand that writers do the same thing; they have all kinds of plot outlines that maybe one day will be a book, or a play, or something like that. One of the things I began accumulating was a lot of waltz tunes—because I happen to love waltzes. Somebody pointed out to me, 'they're not bad, but they sound like Johann Strauss'…with one exception, and that's the waltz that we are to play next. It was called *Belle of the Ball*. This one seemed to be in a more modern style, so that's why the other waltzes are still lying down in the old notebook."

Blue Tango (1951) This melody in tango rhythm became a hit for Anderson in 1952. For many weeks it was the number one piece of popular music in the United States. Additionally, it was the first instrumental recording to sell more than one million copies. Anderson said: "I wrote a melody in a tango rhythm and, since the arrangement was in a blues character in the old jazz style, it seemed appropriate to name the piece *Blue Tango*."

The Bluebells of Scotland (1954) This traditional melody takes on new freshness as a result of Anderson's humorous arrangement which explores tonal colors.

Bugler's Holiday (1954) During a Boston Pops concert, Anderson said: "I've often thought, what would three buglers do on their day off? They would probably kick up their heels and just have a good time all to themselves. So in the next piece, *Bugler's Holiday*, you'll hear some bugle calls that may sound familiar, but you'll also probably realize that they are not played regulation and they wouldn't get away with it on the post."

The Captains and the Kings (1962) This piece was inspired by a quote from Rudyard Kipling's "Recessional": "The tumult and the shouting dies; / The Captains and the Kings depart: / Still stands Thine ancient sacrifice, / An humble and a contrite heart. / Lord God of Hosts, be with us yet, / Lest we forget— lest we forget!" While most marches have two beats in each measure, *The Captains and the Kings* uses changing meter, going from 2/4 to 3/4. The piece was written in two parts: Captains first, Kings second.

China Doll (1951) "*China Doll*, as the title suggests, has a delicate, fragile melody, first played by the oboe, then by the entire orchestra," Anderson said.

Clarinet Candy (1962) Anderson wrote this work as a showpiece for clarinets. He once said in concert: "I've always admired clarinets. I never played one myself. Those of you who know someone who's a clarinetist realize that it has a very low range and it has a very high range. And it's these two ranges that I used in *Clarinet Candy*."

Leroy Anderson at a recording session in 1961 with the clarinet soloists in his *Clarinet Candy*.

Fiddle-Faddle (1947) This piece, featuring violins, is based upon Paganini's *Moto Perpetuo* but in a contemporary style. Anderson said: "The first numbers that I wrote for the Boston Pops concerts featured the strings….Perhaps it's because I happen to be a string player myself. I used to play the double bass, and you might say that I never got over it. Of course, strings are really wonderful instruments because they can play very rapid passages over a long period of time and never get tired, because they don't have to stop to take a breath like the other instruments. Anyway, that's probably why Paganini and other composers wrote very fast numbers for the strings. They called them "moto perpetuo," perpetual motion. So, that was the idea in back of the number that I wrote, except that I didn't call it perpetual motion; since it was a modern piece, I gave it a modern title, *Fiddle-Faddle*."

The First Day of Spring (1954) The French horn is featured in the orchestral original piece which captures the happy expectations of the joys of spring.

Forgotten Dreams (1954) Anderson said that he first thought of *Forgotten Dreams* as a piano solo. "But as I started to play over this thing, it seemed to me that it had more scope to the melody than something that would be just a little simple piano piece. In other words, it needed a little fuller treatment, and it needed an orchestral background. So I developed it into what became *Forgotten Dreams.*"

The Girl in Satin (1953) This melodic piece was written in a tango rhythm. Anderson commented during a radio program: "I personally feel that *Blue Tango* is a splendid piece of music, otherwise I would have thrown it into the waste basket and not tried to find a publisher and record it. But as a composer I do not have any clue why the audience likes it so much better than my other tango, *The Girl in Satin*, which in my opinion is as beautiful."

The Golden Years (1962) This ballad is characterized by a triumphant melody and warm romanticism.

Governor Bradford March (1948) Anderson included this piece in a catalog of his works that he compiled in 1970, even though the piece had not been published. This piano solo transcription by the composer is published for the first time in this collection. This march is named after Robert Bradford who served as Massachusetts Governor from 1947 to 1949.

Home Stretch (1962) Anderson described *Home Stretch* as a piece that expresses "some of the excitement that you feel when the horses come galloping down the last stretch."

Horse and Buggy (1951) Four percussion players help create a convincing depiction of this early form of transportation.

Jazz Legato (1938) Written as a companion piece to *Jazz Pizzicato*, here the violins are bowed in a legato style.

Jazz Pizzicato (1938) Anderson's first piece featured pizzicato strings with jazz rhythms. "After writing this number, I added a companion piece which, in contrast, is played with the bow in a legato style and is called, also appropriately, *Jazz Legato.*"

Lady in Waiting (1959) This was the lyrical opening of the second act of the musical, *Goldilocks*.

An Old-Fashioned Song (1965) In the mid-1960s Anderson began writing a series of musical studies for beginning piano students. They were all for one piano for four hands, for a student and teacher to play together. He wrote one simple yet charming piece for piano solo and called it, *An Old-Fashioned Song*. It is published here for the first time.

The Penny-Whistle Song (1951) Three flutes are featured in this upbeat miniature. Anderson said: "I've spent hours wracking my brains, going over and over again in my mind, away from the piano, just thinking it over as if I were listening to it, whether the modulation should be two measures or four measures

between different sections because I feel every measure has to count. I do remember spending four days, having written *The Penny-Whistle Song*, trying to get an introduction. I just couldn't get an introduction. I spent four days at it and finally came up with the four-measure introduction. This is what you have to do when you are writing smaller numbers."

The Phantom Regiment (1951) Anderson described this work as "a sort of imaginative idea of a phantom regiment. What kind of regiment it is, I don't know. I'm just suggesting it's some sort of body of people who are marching for some purpose, and I'm going to leave it up to you to decide exactly what that is."

Plink, Plank, Plunk! (1951) This perky number is played by the string section plucking the strings rather than by using their bows. Anderson said: "Although I started my career as an organist, later on I played mainly string bass in orchestras. For everyone writing orchestral pieces, playing a string instrument is an excellent experience, since one acquires a valuable technical knowledge of the most important part of the orchestra. As a bass player I got first hand knowledge of the resources of a string orchestra and became particularly interested in the use of the pizzicato, which is very often neglected by composers. As an example of how one can use the pizzicato, I wrote a little piece with the title *Plink, Plank, Plunk!* The string players lay down their bows and from the beginning to the end of the piece, pluck the strings of their instruments."

Promenade (1945) The brisk walking theme, first played by muted solo trumpet, is followed by a flowing middle section and then returns with the full orchestra playing a broad finale. Anderson said that this piece and *Serenata* both started with a fragment of melody. "From the first notes the melodic line grew into a full melody with harmonic and rhythmic background,

Leroy Anderson in the 1950s.

Leroy Anderson in the 1960s

then other sections were added, and an introduction and a coda were worked out to make a well-rounded composition, and finally I added a title that seemed best to identify the music."

Pyramid Dance (1959) This brilliant finale of Anderson's musical, *Goldilocks*, features a melody appropriate for an Egyptian setting.

Sandpaper Ballet (1954) This captivating waltz for orchestra incorporates the sounds of three grades of sandpaper. Anderson recalled: "Many years ago while the soft shoe dance was still popular in vaudeville, sometimes dancers would sprinkle sand on the stage to create a crackling sound while performing. The drummers imitated this sound by attaching sandpaper on wooden blocks which they rubbed rhythmically against each other. This was the background for my piece *Sandpaper Ballet*. The sandpaper-covered blocks are in this case imitated by two drummers. They use sandpaper in three different strengths— coarse, medium and fine—to create different effects."

Saraband (1948) The 18th century sarabande dance is updated with the flavor of a modern fox-trot in this combination of past and present. Anderson commented: "I have often wondered if our modern popular dance forms, such as the fox-trot and rhumba, will be used by composers two centuries from now as much as the 18th century classical dances are used by composers of the present day. The gigue, hornpipe, and pavane of the classical suites are still used today, but with modern styles. In the setting of *Saraband*, I have kept the slow triple rhythm of the classical saraband in the melody, but the underlying rhythm has been doubled in tempo to produce the effect of the modern fox-trot. In the middle section, however, the slow triple rhythm is heard alone for a while, like an echo of the past, but then the doubled rhythm is resumed."

Serenata (1947) Anderson said that in writing *Serenata*, "I began with the flowing melody you hear as the main section. Then, since this main part was in a major key with a very broad melody, the music seemed to call for something to introduce it in a minor key, so I wrote the first section with fast repeated notes. When the whole thing was put together with a beguine rhythm as a background, it seemed to me to sound like a Latin-American serenade, so I added the Spanish title *Serenata*."

Sleigh Ride (1948) This Christmas season standard conveys a vivid picture of a crisp winter day on a snowy country road, complete with trotting horse, whip, and sleigh bells. Anderson recalled composing this piece: "*Sleigh Ride* was one of the first things I wrote when I got out of the Army and moved to Woodbury, Connecticut. Actually, I first came here in 1946. There was a housing shortage then, and my mother-in-law was living up here and had a cottage that was vacant. So since we had no other place to go, we packed our 14-month old daughter plus the upright piano, and came on up here to Woodbury. During that first summer that we were here, I started *Fiddle Faddle*. I didn't finish that until the following winter, and *Sleigh Ride* and *Serenata*. And *Sleigh Ride*, I remember, was just an idea because it was just a pictorial thing, it wasn't necessarily Christmas music, and it was written during the heat wave."

Leroy Anderson, conductor of the Harvard University Band in 1929.

Song of the Bells (1953) This whirling, infectious waltz features orchestral bells and chimes. In a radio interview, Anderson commented: "In music encyclopedias, bells are mentioned as very effective instruments especially for dramatic and theater music. Unfortunately, there are only a few composers who are able to write music such as the *Symphonie Fantastique* by Berlioz or an opera like *Parsifal*. In both cases, bells are used to create a sense of reality. One music encyclopedia concludes rather laconically that a composer very rarely has an opportunity to write a piece with bell-accompaniment. I once wrote a waltz, of which the first few notes, when played, sounded like bells, and I asked myself why bells are mainly used only with church scenes, religious themes or grandiose festive events. Why should bells not be used simply because of their beautiful sound? The result was a waltz with the title *Song of the Bells*. Bells are conventionally not connected with a waltz. In the middle part, a glockenspiel is added to the bells, both playing a duet. The small glockenspiel accompanies the slow notes of the big bells with fast notes."

Summer Skies (1953) This work paints an evocative picture of a bright, sunny day during which the sky, at times, is filled with passing clouds.

The Syncopated Clock (1945) This was the first musical composition based on a clock that beats to a syncopated rhythm. When he was asked, which do you think of first, the title or the composition, Anderson answered, "Well, actually, I do both. In certain cases, such as *The Syncopated Clock*, I thought of the title, as it came to me, because it incorporated an idea that I thought could be expressed in music. I noticed that there have been hundreds and hundreds, if not thousands, of tunes about clocks. It suddenly struck me that all these clocks were regular clocks, such as you hear everywhere. No one had written a musical composition based on a syncopated clock, that is, a clock that beats to a syncopated rhythm. And the idea struck me as an attractive one, and I then sat down and wrote the music to go with the title."

Town House Maxixe (1959) This was based on a dance from Brazil that was popular during the mid-1900s. Anderson wrote it to accompany the silent film-era action of the musical, *Goldilocks*.

A Trumpeter's Lullaby (1949) This lullaby is a favorite for trumpeters. Although the melody is based on bugle call notes and figures idiomatic to the trumpet, this piece creates the mood of a lullaby. During a concert, Anderson said that *Trumpeter's Lullaby* had its beginning backstage at Symphony Hall in Boston. "In addition to composing and conducting, I was arranger for the Boston Pops Orchestra for a number of years. After one of the concerts I was sitting, talking with the conductor, Arthur Fiedler, and the first trumpet of the Boston Pops, Roger Voisin. Suddenly, Roger Voisin asked me why I didn't write a trumpet solo for him to play with the orchestra that would be different from traditional trumpet solos which are all loud, martial or triumphant. After thinking it over, it

occurred to me that I had never heard a lullaby for trumpet, so I set out to write one—with a quiet melody based on bugle notes played by the trumpet and with the rest of the orchestra playing a lullaby background."

Turn Ye to Me (1954) An old highland tune that is effectively presented by the strings in the orchestra.

The Typewriter (1950) This is a study in musical fun, featuring a real typewriter as the solo instrument. The piano solo version combines the typewriter sounds and the orchestral accompaniment.

The Waltzing Cat (1950) At a concert Anderson introduced *The Waltzing Cat*: "If, as you listen to the music, you imagine something like Puss 'n Boots at a fancy dress ball, that is just about what the composer had in mind."

1972 PBS "Evening at Pops" with Leroy Anderson conducting the Boston Pops.

The official Leroy Anderson Web site can be found at www.leroyanderson.com.

This site was created by Kurt Anderson, General Manager of WMNR, a public radio station in Connecticut, and one of four children of Leroy Anderson.

Arietta

Leroy Anderson

Balladette

Leroy Anderson

Belle of the Ball

Leroy Anderson

Blue Tango

Leroy Anderson

Bugler's Holiday

Leroy Anderson

The Bluebells of Scotland

(from the "Scottish Suite")

Leroy Anderson

China Doll

Leroy Anderson

The Captains and the Kings

Leroy Anderson

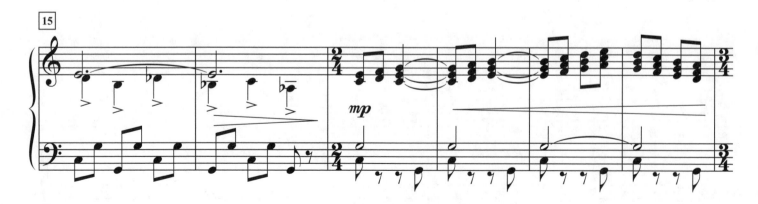

Clarinet Candy

Leroy Anderson

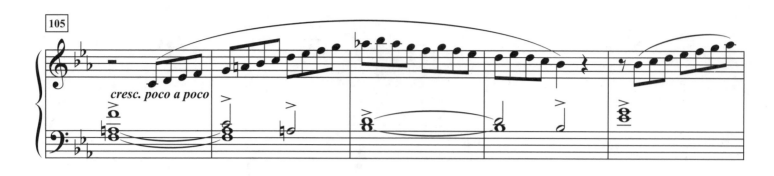

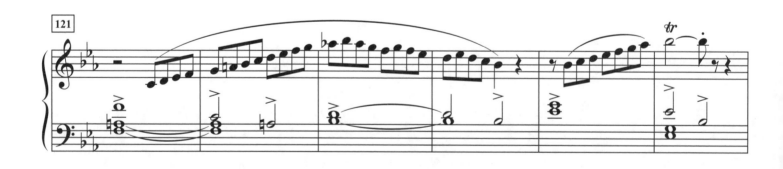

Fiddle-Faddle

Leroy Anderson

The First Day of Spring

Leroy Anderson

Forgotten Dreams

Leroy Anderson

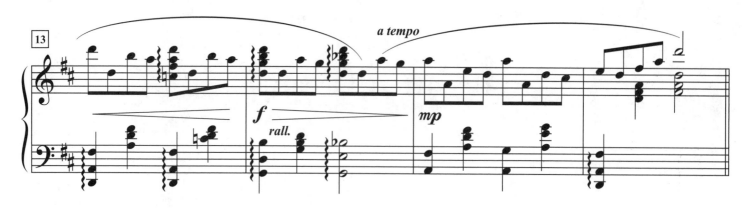

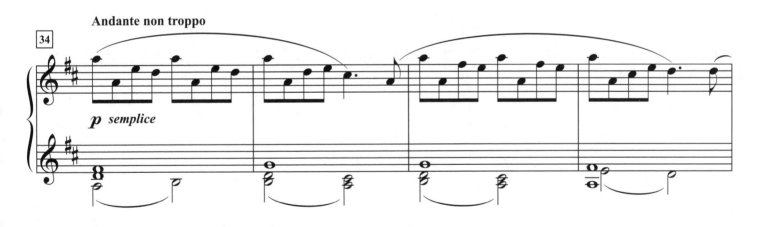

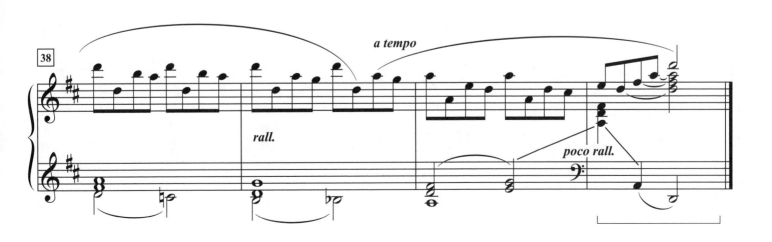

The Girl in Satin

Leroy Anderson

Governor Bradford March

Leroy Anderson

The Golden Years

Leroy Anderson

Tempo I

Home Stretch

Leroy Anderson

Horse and Buggy

Leroy Anderson

An Old-Fashioned Song

Leroy Anderson

Jazz Legato

Leroy Anderson

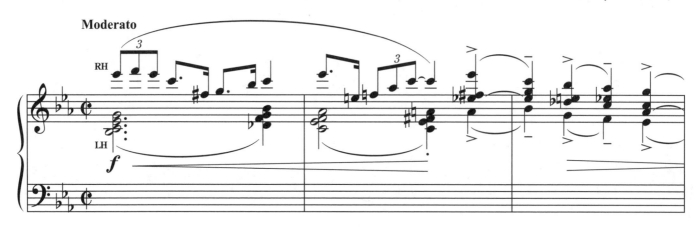

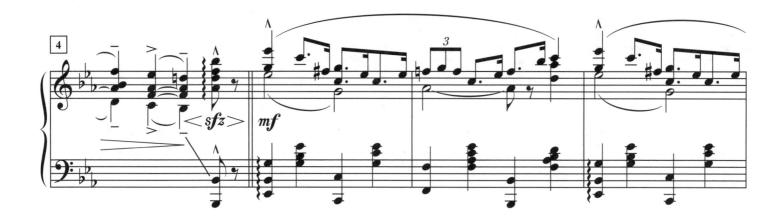

Jazz Pizzicato

Leroy Anderson

Lady in Waiting

From Walter and Jean Kerr, Joan Ford and Leroy Anderson's "Goldilocks"

Music by Leroy Anderson

The Penny-Whistle Song

Leroy Anderson

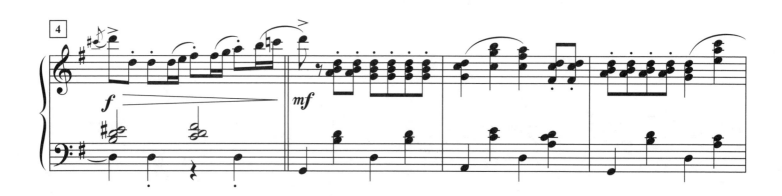

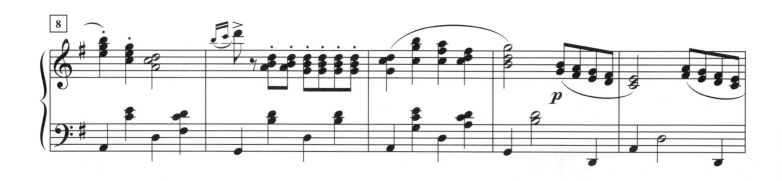

The Phantom Regiment

Leroy Anderson

Plink, Plank, Plunk!

Leroy Anderson

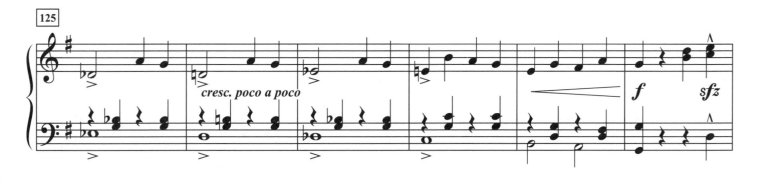

Pyramid Dance
(Heart of Stone)
From Walter and Jean Kerr, Joan Ford and Leroy Anderson's "Goldilocks"

Music by Leroy Anderson

Promenade

Leroy Anderson

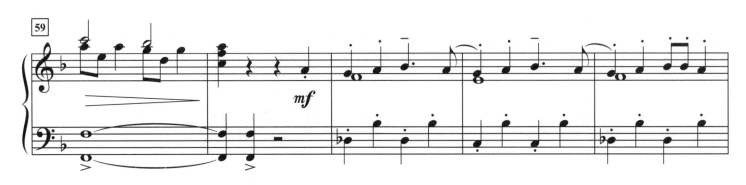

Saraband

Leroy Anderson

Sandpaper Ballet

Leroy Anderson

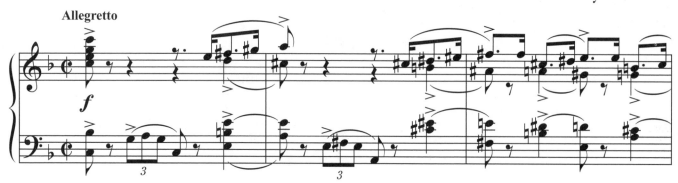

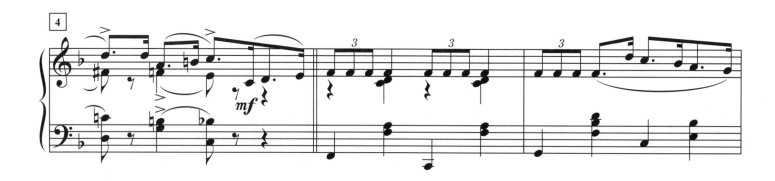

Serenata

Leroy Anderson

Sleigh Ride

Leroy Anderson

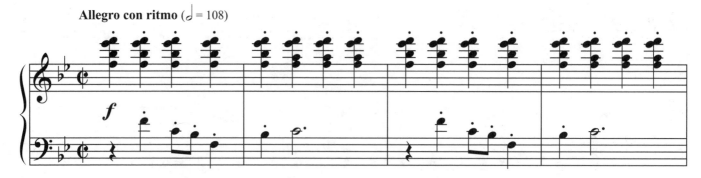

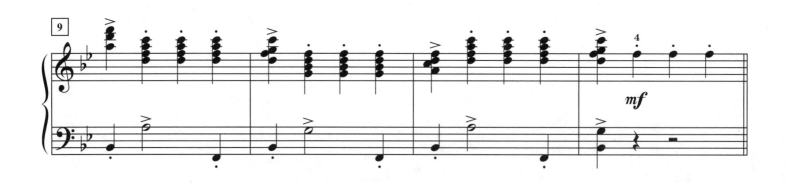

Song of the Bells

Leroy Anderson

The Syncopated Clock

Leroy Anderson

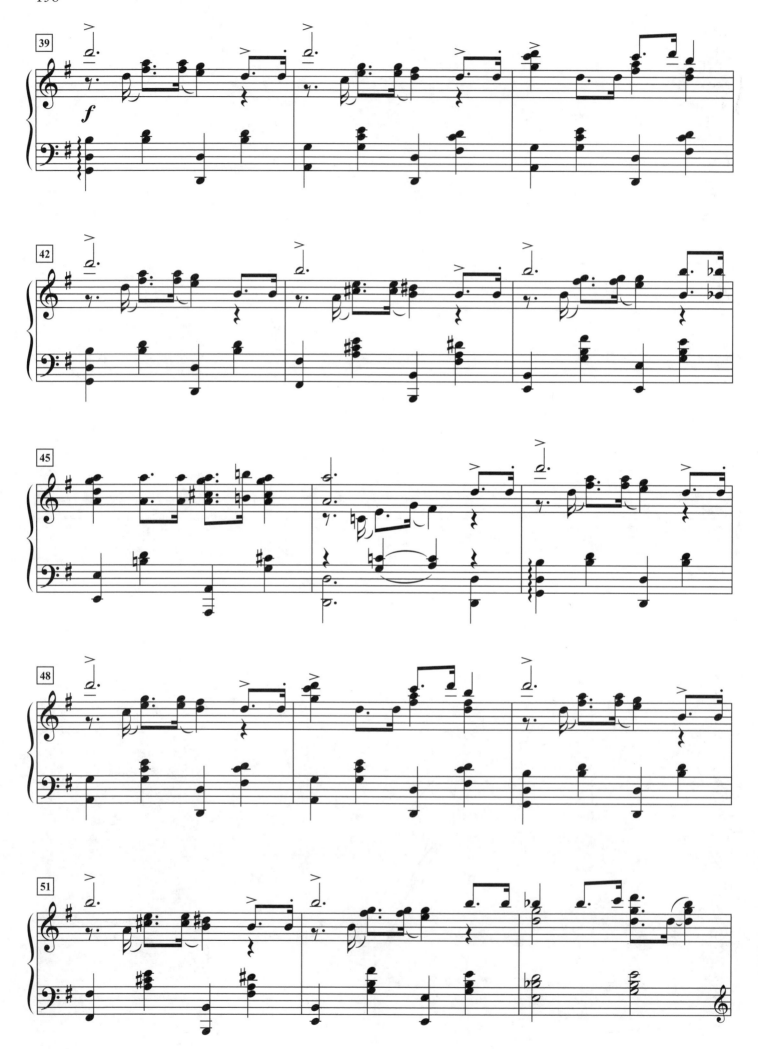

Summer Skies

Leroy Anderson

Turn Ye to Me
(from the "Scottish Suite")

Leroy Anderson

Town House Maxixe

From Walter and Jean Kerr, Joan Ford and Leroy Anderson's "Goldilocks"

Music by Leroy Anderson

A Trumpeter's Lullaby

Leroy Anderson

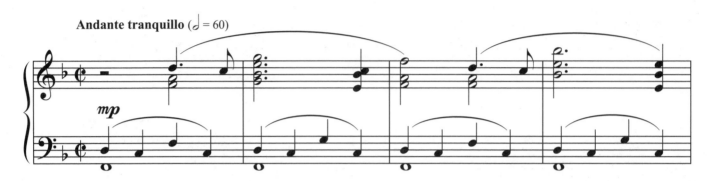

The Typewriter

Leroy Anderson

The Waltzing Cat

Leroy Anderson

181

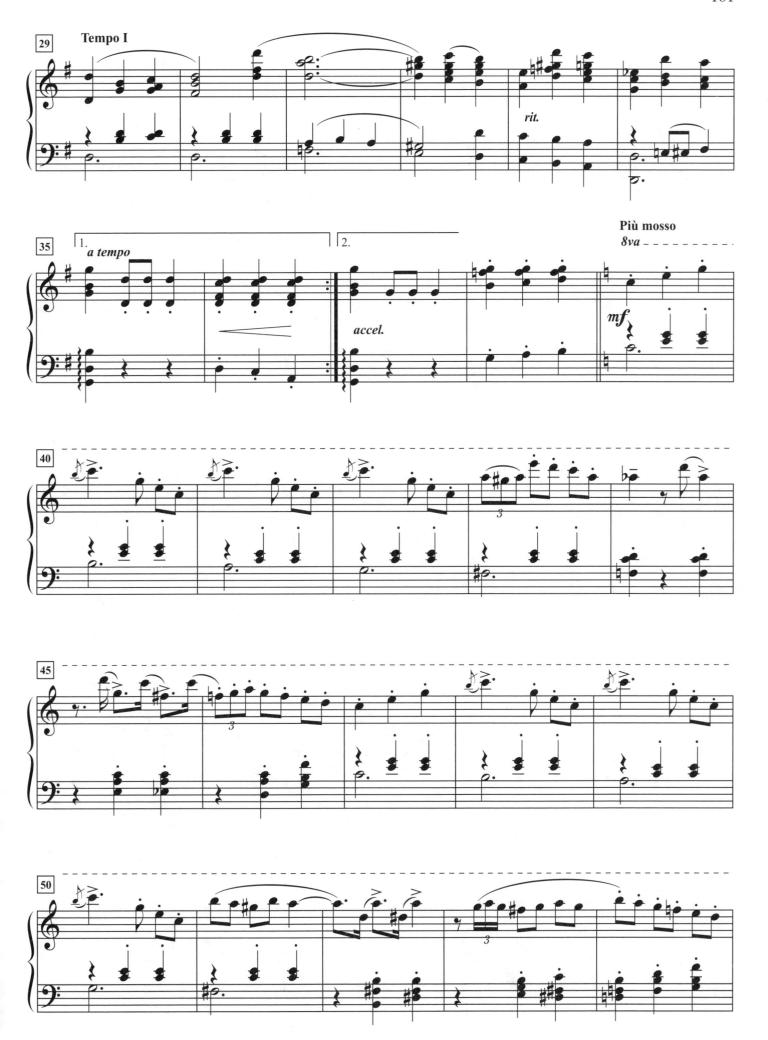